Papa Moll at the Swiss Museum of Transport

Publisher: Globi Publishing
Creator of the character Papa Moll: Edith Jonas
Story and illustrations: Rolf Meier
Story and text: Jürg Lendenmann
English translation: David Levine

Discover the Swiss Museum of Transport with the Moll Family

Join Papa Moll and his whole family for amusing adventures in the Transport Museum. Our Museum brings the exciting story of transportation to life with interactive exhibits focusing on the development of transportation and mobility. We show you the history of travel by road, rail, in and under the water, as well as in the air and outer space. The exhibits are continually renewed and improved. So don't be too surprised if you encounter new attractions on your next visit!

We wish you an enjoyable 'Voyage of Discovery' and look forward to your visit.

Did you know…

… that the Swiss Museum of Transport's cinema screen is the largest in the country? It's 21 meters wide and 19 meters high.
… that more than 3000 objects are on display?
… that the Transport Museum is the most visited museum in Switzerland?
… that the Swissarena is the world's only walkable satellite photo of an entire country?
… that there is enough space in the Arena (museum courtyard) for six helicopters to land or 1500 motorcycles to park?
… that the glass facade of the entrance building is covered with over 5000 different wheels, steering wheels, hubcaps, airplane and ship propellers?

Open 365 days a year!

Swiss Museum of Transport
Lidostrasse 5, CH-6006 Lucerne

www.verkehrshaus.ch
www.filmtheater.ch

Opening hours:
Summer Time 10 – 18 h
Winter Time 10 – 17 h

Papa Moll at the Swiss Museum of Transport

Copyright © 2011
Globi Verlag, Imprint der
Orell Füssli Verlag AG, 8036 Zurich, Switzerland
www.globi.ch

English Edition
1. Edition
ISBN 978-3-85703-027-7

Environmentally friendly printing and packaging.

2011
Printed by: Kösel GmbH & Co. KG

They want fun and like to learn:
that's why the Molls went to Lucerne!
The Museum of Transport's got
fun and learning in one spot!

Papa Moll begins the day
on the aerial cable way.
Smoothly rising to great heights,
Papa Moll can see the sights!

Mama Moll's at the window
of 'Albergo Svizzero'.
She has got a friendly look,
and hopes that you enjoy this book!

Fritz and **Evi** are afloat,
on the deck of the steam boat.
Willy rides that fast train there.
He stuck his head out for fresh air.

Chips the dog is last, not least.
He's a clever little beast!
Full of tricks and full of fun,
he keeps his family on the run!

Papa Moll

Off to the Swiss Museum of Transport!

1 Washing every pot and pan,
each dish and plate get spick and span!
The chore is very nearly done,
Teamwork makes the washing fun!

2 Then suddenly the dish-wash team
is interrupted by a scream:
Papa Moll and his good wife
hear the sound of children's strife.

3 'I'll go check and see what's wrong',
says Papa Moll, 'I won't be long.'
Straight to the children's room he strides,
and hears loud shouting from all sides.

4 He roughly opens up the door.
'Are you children playing war?
It's as loud as a big riot!
Really, children! Please be quiet!'

5 'My "Crocodile" is the best!'
shouts Fritz, 'It clearly beats the rest!'
'No!' screams Willy, 'No more tricks!
The best is my "Ae 6/6"!'

6 Evi's eyes are getting narrow:
'Nothing beats my cool "Red Arrow"!'
Papa Moll is now confused
by the words his children used.

7 'When I was young, I was the same,
and knew each engine by its name!'
Then Moll remembers way on back
each locomotive on the track.

8 And now he sees his kids are keen
to learn about the Swiss train scene.
'There must be some place we can go
to teach them what they want to know!'

9 A smile then lights up his face:
'I know just the perfect place!
There's a spot of the right sort:
The Swiss Museum of Transport!'

Papa Moll

So Many Ways to Go

1   The early bird, as some folks say,
    gets the worm without delay.
    There's no time for hesitation
    at the city's main train station.

2   'Early risers get to see
    more in life, undoubtedly'
    said Papa Moll and they agree.
    The kids all smile eagerly.

3   'The Museum is our next goal,
    tickets please,' says Papa Moll.
    'Two adults with children three,
    plus Chips, completes the family.'

4 The ticket seller wants to know
how the Molls would like to go.
'From Lucerne by bus, boat, train?'
'The boat!' cries Willy, 'that's quite plain!'

5 Evi answers, 'No! No! No!
the boat is not the way to go!
Chips gets queasy out at sea,
we must go there separately!'

6 Fritz has got a clever brain,
and cries, 'Let Chips ride on the train!
He always takes the train, you see,
and loves to sit with Mom and me!'

7 Moll approves of Fritz's plan:
'We need tickets, my good man!
One and a half plus dog by rail,
the others on the ship will sail!'

8 'The other way, on the trip back,
two kids plus dog will go by track.
One and a half the ship will take
across Lucerne's most scenic Lake.'

9 It was all quite complicated;
finally it's calculated!
All the tickets for this band,
Moll has got them in his hand!

Papa Moll

Chips, the Actor

1 Now the Molls are on the go
with the 'InterRegio'
There is so much here to be seen:
Lakes of blue and hills of green.

2 In Lucerne, the big ship's moored.
The sailors call out, 'All aboard!'
Then it's time to wave, 'Bye-bye!'
Poor Chips yelps out a nervous cry.

3 To the S3 train they run,
carrying the little one.
The train is ready, all climb on,
the engine starts and then they're gone.

4　What is this that they now hear?
　　Children's voices, very near.
　　Kids on a field trip out of school,
　　to the Museum: that's very cool!

5　'Look! This doggie is so sweet!'
　　'Let's give him a tasty treat!'
　　As the train rolls down the tracks,
　　the kids feed Chips with junk food snacks!

6　A mere eight minutes lasts the ride
　　along Lucerne's lovely lake side.
　　Greedy Chips eats all the way.
　　'We're almost there!' shouts Fritz, 'Hooray!'

7　Chips has eaten much too much
　　chocolate, candy, chips and such.
　　A short walk's all he has to take,
　　but Chips has got a stomach ache!

8　Mama Moll scolds, 'Chips, be quiet!
　　You should go on a strict diet!'
　　But then, it seems that Chips feels fine,
　　and starts to bark and stops to whine.

9　Chips is pleased and quite delighted
　　now his family's re-united.
　　His recovery was quick.
　　Chips was never really sick!

Papa Moll

A Tight Squeeze

1 At the Museum, the entrance fees
reflect the needs of families.
'For us it is the Family Rate,'
says Papa Moll, 'that is just great!'

2 'This will be the best of days!'
he continues, as he pays.
The ticket woman does not see
how Chips has waited patiently.

3 She didn't see the dog and so,
she didn't say that Chips can't go.
The sign is absolutely clear:
'Dogs are not allowed in here!'

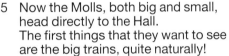

4 Although the guard has eagle eyes,
he didn't even realize
that Chips has entered sneakily.
Behind his back he cannot see!

5 Now the Molls, both big and small,
head directly to the Hall.
The first things that they want to see
are the big trains, quite naturally!

6 Papa Moll, with a big smile,
strolls right up to the turnstile.
Inserts his ticket in the slot,
tries to walk through, but he cannot!

7 Poor Papa Moll is out of luck,
He can't get out. He's gotten stuck!
Trapped in the turnstile, really tight;
it just won't budge, try as he might!

8 'The turnstile's broken now, I fear!
I might be stuck here for a year!'
Again he tries to break out free.
He won't escape this easily!

9 They push and pull him valiantly,
until Poor Moll is finally free.
The turnstile opens with a 'click',
teamwork, again, has done the trick!

Papa Moll

Where's the Dog?

1 And what of Chips in the meanwhile?
   Small dogs aren't stopped by a turnstile.
   Chips just trotted right on through,
   as if he'd nothing else to do.

2 But just then, the Museum Guard
   turns around and looks real hard.
   Now what was that? It sure looked weird:
   a dog's tail just has disappeared!

3 'You come back here!' he shouts loud,
   'Dogs are strictly not allowed!'
   But Chips is fast as well as cute,
   He's got the guard in hot pursuit.

4 'Wow! Look at this "Crocodile"!
   This engine always makes me smile.'
   Excited eyes are open wide,
   they view the engine from each side.

5 'This "Landi" Locomotive here
   is quite impressive, that is clear.
   Perhaps the largest in the Hall,
   it makes the "Croc" there seem quite small.'

6 Now Mr Steiner rushes by,
   a hunter's gleam is in his eye.
   Now he's bewildered. Is this fair?
   The dog has vanished in thin air!

7 Willy's admiration's keen
   as he discusses the machine.
   Fritz says, '"Be 6/8":
   built in the twenties, this is great!'

8 The guard seeks Chips, where can he be?
   'Just trains and kids are all I see!'
   Searching every nook and cranny,
   he can't find that dog, now can he?

9 After scouring the whole Hall,
   He thinks that there's no dog at all.
   So he gives up and walks away.
   He'll find that dog another day!

Papa Moll

Tickets, Please!

1 Being small has got its perks,
Chips the dog knows how this works.
He fits in the smallest spaces
and can go all kinds of places!

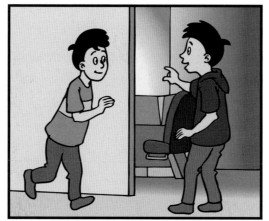

2 Fritz and Willy stroll on through
the displays ,til they come to
the Museum's new Simulator.
Astonishment could not be greater!

3 Thanks to the Simulator's screen,
it feels like you drive the machine!
It's the closest you can get,
it's like a giant toy train set!

4   When Papa Moll comes strolling in,
his face is lit up with a grin.
'My childhood dream can now come true!
I get to drive this big choo-choo!'

5   He steers the train with utmost care,
and doesn't see three figures there.
His kids are hiding out of sight.
'We'll give our Dad an awful fright!'

6   Fritz makes his voice go gruff and low.
He does not want his Dad to know
that this is one of his new pranks:
'Tickets, please, Sir! Many thanks!'

7   Poor Moll is taken by surprise
and leaps right up with great big eyes.
He grabs his wallet in a flash.
But there's no ticket, only cash.

8   He holds his wallet in his hand
and slowly starts to understand.
'This is crazy! It's insane!
This is not a real life train!'

9   'Ha! Ha! Ha! We fooled you, Dad!'
Papa Moll is far from mad.
In fact he chortles, 'Kids, well done!
You really know how to have fun!'

Papa Moll

Chips Hunts a Motorcycle

Ausfahrt: Englisch = Exit

1   The family Moll is full of cheer.
    They've quite enjoyed what they've done here.
    No locomotive has been missed.
    Now seeing cars is on their list.

2   From floor to ceiling in the hall
    stands a mighty shelf so tall.
    Old vehicles are on display;
    things with wheels from yesterday.

3   On this shelf are stacks and stacks
    of bikes and cars displayed on racks.
    Motorcycles, coaches, too,
    all vehicles no longer new.

4   A parking robot moves the racks
    up and down along the tracks.
    A button push is all they need:
    'Me first! Me first!' the children plead.

5   The two Moll boys prepare themselves
    to push the buttons for the shelves.
    A motorbike is what they choose,
    They want to win, they hate to lose!

6   The visitors determine which
    rack's selected with a switch.
    See them pressing: Click! Click! Click!
    The most pressed rack will make the pick.

7   The boys' hard work has been rewarded,
    and their choice among assorted
    vehicles has won the test:
    a vintage Harley! That's the best!

8   What is this that Chips now feels?
    Dogs like to chase things with two wheels!
    'I can catch this bike' thinks Chips;
    under the barricade he slips.

9   Now Chips is barking at the bike
    It's funny, and the children like
    to watch the dog behave this way.
    They think it's part of the display!

Papa Moll

Easy Rider

1   Poor little Chips is in harm's way,
    Papa Moll calls in dismay,
    'Chips, my puppy! Please come back!
    You're in danger on that rack!'

2   'There is but one thing I must do!'
    thinks Moll, 'I'm off to the rescue!'
    He doesn't wait, he doesn't stop:
    Chips went bottom, Moll goes top!

3   Moll then calls his dog by name,
    but Chips thinks this is all a game!
    Papa Moll could search all week;
    Chips thinks that it's 'Hide and Seek'.

4 Now the rack begins to rise.
Chips is taken by surprise.
He's afraid and jumps aside,
leaving Moll alone to ride!

5 The rack is moving with a sway
to put the motor bike away.
Moll is knocked right off his feet,
and falls into the side-car seat!

6 Poor Papa Moll just can't get out.
Should he wait or should he shout?
See the worry on his face:
'I can't live in a glass case!'

7 This gives Mama Moll a fright,
'I must try to set things right!'
she says, as Moll moves up the wall,
'This doesn't look too good at all!'

8 'Evi, catch our dog somehow.
I will go for help right now!
I never thought I'd lose someone
to a Harley-Davidson!'

9 Poor Papa Moll is sitting tight
on display still in plain sight.
Mama goes, fast as she can,
to fetch assistance for her man.

Papa Moll

A Solemn Oath

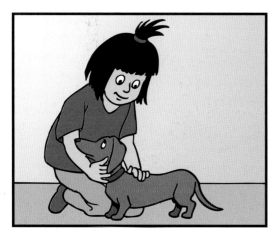

1 Evi finds her little pup,
   pets his back to cheer him up.
   Chips gives out a grateful yelp,
   Mama's gone to look for help.

2 Mama runs and goes to find
   the guard: 'Please help if you don't mind.
   Moll is stuck and we all worry!
   In a Harley! Can you hurry?'

3 High up in the Auto-Hall
   Moll's stuck in the display wall.
   No longer in a jolly mood,
   he simply waits to be rescued.

4 Steiner runs to the control,
to push the switch that saves old Moll.
A click and then he comes back down.
The 'Easy Rider's' on the ground.

5 And so ended Moll's 'joyride':
nothing injured but his pride!
And lands upon his own two feet.
He squeezes out of the tight seat.

6 'It's nice to see you here so soon,
did you try to reach the moon?'
Mama's joke makes them all laugh,
(except for one man on the staff).

7 Mr Steiner, museum guard,
looks at Papa Moll quite hard.
'Mr Moll, you've gone too far,
don't ride in any bike or car!'

8 Papa Moll now sinks his head,
see, his cheeks are getting red!
He's ashamed of what he's done:
a fool in front of everyone!

9 Moll is filled with true regret,
'I've been bad and won't forget:
the rules I promise to obey,
and never enter the display!'

Papa Moll

Pride before the Fall

1 'Papa Moll, your Harley ride,
was anything but dignified!
This is no place to fool around,
but we're so glad you're safe and sound!'

2 'There's another sort of ride,
a crash test car that can collide!
Mama Moll, now answer me,
could you crash with dignity?'

3 Mama Moll says, 'Yes, I could.
A bit of fun would do me good!
I'll take the boys along with me.
There's no problem, you will see!'

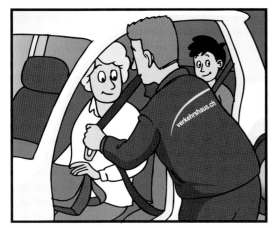

4 Mama and the boys climb in
to take the crash car for a spin.
First the seatbelts are pulled tight:
'Safety First' of course, that's right!

5 'You should leave your bag with me,
that's the crash-test policy!'
But Mama Moll says: 'Sorry, no!
My bag comes with me where I go'.

6 The crash car starts and off they go,
not too fast, but not too slow.
Soon they go thirteen an hour,
prepare to crash with all that power!

7 Bang, they stop with a hard jerk,
they're grateful that the seatbelts work!
Mama holds the bag, but still...
All the contents? Out they spill!

8 Everything that was inside,
has flown out from the crash test ride.
All her candy, combs and keys,
all her pens and vanities!

9 Papa Moll helps her collect
everything but self-respect!
Now it seems that he and she
both have equal dignity!

Papa Moll

Double Plunge

1   They go out for some fresh air,
    little Evi's waiting there.
    Joyful Chips just barks like mad,
    to see his family makes him glad.

2   Chips hops around and wags his tail.
    Will the poor dog end up in jail?
    The guard has seen him and is near,
    poor Chips lets out a yelp of fear.

3   'Catch that mutt! No dogs allowed!'
    shouts Mr Steiner very loud!
    'I'll grab that dog' we hear Moll say.
    But Chips is fast and gets away.

4 'A kickboard is just what I need!
   These two wheels will give me speed!'
   Determination on his face,
   Moll embarks upon the chase.

5 'Fetch the dog... and not the stick?'
   Chips finds this a funny trick!
   He begins to bark and run:
   'Catch me! Catch me! This is fun!'

6 Steiner takes a kickboard, too.
   'Watch out, dog! I will catch you!'
   Of course the children want to see,
   and join the action eagerly.

7 Chips has stopped quick as a wink,
   Moll rolls up right to the brink.
   He can stop in time, oh my!
   And so he's able to keep dry.

8 But the guard makes a mistake,
   and steps too late upon the brake.
   He's still going at full rate,
   can Moll stop him? It's too late!

9 It all happens in a flash:
   Moll and guard both make a splash,
   in the chase of Chips the Pup,
   two men embarrassed, all washed up!

1 Moll and Steiner: both are wet
because they tried to catch Moll's pet.
They're in the water, but not hurt.
Drenched are trousers, shoes and shirt.

2 They fell in, and then thereafter
were a great source of much laughter.
The restaurant guests watched them collide,
and gather round the basin's side.

3 Now a group of people gawk
and laugh and point and joke and talk
about the clever little hound,
who nearly got two grown men drowned.

4 The guard looks Moll right in the eyes
   and says: 'I must apologize!'
   'Don't worry now', Moll says to him,
   'I quite enjoyed our little swim.'

5 'I am sorry' Steiner said,
   as his cheeks are turning red.
   'I am ashamed of the whole thing,
   in fact, it is embarassing!'

6 Moll stands up a dripping mess,
   and says 'So sorry for this stress.
   I guess our visit's over now,
   I need to dry my clothes somehow.'

7 Steiner says 'No need to fret,
   soon we'll be no longer wet!
   In our own infirmary
   there is a dryer for laundry.'

8 'This has happened here before,
   now follow me right through this door.'
   And it's true, he is no liar,
   in this room is a clothes dryer.

9 'Put these on `til your clothes dry.'
   'Thank you nurse, that's kind. Goodbye.'
   Fresh bathrobes for the two wet men,
   who sit and start to chat right then.

Papa Moll

Brains over Brawn

1   'This might take a little while,'
Mama Moll says with a smile,
'There's no need to stand and stare,
the Arena is right there.'

2   All three children start to run,
Chips wants to join in the fun.
'No, Chips, it's a dog-free zone,
the children will go there alone!'

3   Evi, Willy, also Fritz
run away while poor Chips sits.
The Arena's full of treats.
It's where children can build streets!

4 It's a big construction site
   where kids can build to their delight.
   Fritz is really much in luck;
   see him playing with a truck.

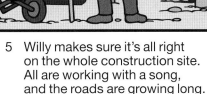

5 Willy makes sure it's all right
   on the whole construction site.
   All are working with a song,
   and the roads are growing long.

6 Then a rather nasty boy
   comes to ruin the kids' joy.
   'You're the sons and you're the daughter
   of that dumbie in the water!'

7 That really wasn't very nice,
   then Willy recalls Moll's advice:
   brains over brawn's the way to go'
   'My Dad is quite renowned, you know'.

8 'My father's swum the seven seas,
   from Singapore to Hebrides!'
   He is honoured world wide,
   a hero's heart, his children's pride!

9 'And next year he will even fly
   to the moon up in the sky!'
   The bully can't believe his ears
   and stands there speechless, close to tears.

Papa Moll

All's Well that Ends Well

1. The two men in the bathrobes chat
   cheerfully of this and that.
   Moll and the guard are now good friends,
   that's almost how the story ends.

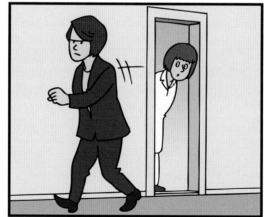

2. News of the wild kickboard show
   has reached the museum's CEO.
   Because the rules here have been bent,
   he sends along his assistant.

3. Ms Smith now walks into the room,
   with a dark look full of gloom.
   'The circus number that you guys
   pulled off was neither safe nor wise!'

4 'It was the dog! We're innocent!'
said Steiner to the assistant.
'We didn't see the 'No Dogs' sign'
said Moll, 'the blame cannot be mine!'

5 'A dog? What dog?' she asks the men,
And Chips and Mama come in then.
'Hello', said Mama, 'I can see,
that you've got charming company!'

6 'Oh, my! This dog is truly sweet!'
Ms Smith now sees that Chips is neat.
Chips likes her too, and so it went
that no one got a punishment.

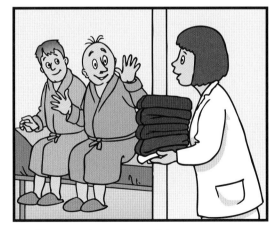

7 'About 'No Dogs' we did not know,
I think the sign was hung too low'
Mama Moll told assistant
'Really now, no harm was meant.'

8 Ms Smith says ,'It's all ok,
I hope that you enjoy your stay!
You can leave the dog with me,
I'll care for him happily.'

9 The men let out a joyful cry,
at last their clothes are nice and dry.
'We can go on as before!'
They laugh as they go out the door.

Papa Moll

Traffic Jam

1 Moll bids farewell to his new friend,
'That was fun, but now I'll spend
the rest of this fine afternoon
with my family! See you soon!'

2 The children greet him with delight:
'Hey, there! Pop! Are you all right?'
'I'm dry again, come on let's go!
We've still a lot to see, you know!'

3 On the way to the next hall
The children see an open mall
filled with cars for kids to steer,
'We can have more fun right here!'

4 The man in charge now wants to take
his long awaited luncheon break.
A friendly smile on his face,
Moll offers him to take his place.

5 The man agrees with gratitude,
and Moll starts with good attittude.
'I'll direct the traffic flow,
don't worry Sir, now you can go.'

6 'Children! Your attention, please!
It's time for me to mention these
traffic signs that I will make:
Stop, slow down, accelerate.'

7 Papa Moll, the traffic cop,
signs for kids to go and stop.
He happily gives sign and sign
with lots of cheer but no design.

8 Although his traffic signs are new,
the children follow well and true.
Despite this fact, to Moll's surprise,
the traffic starts to crystalize.

9 'What kind of traffic cop I am,
I've just made one big traffic jam!'
In the middle, Moll must shout:
'Somebody! Please get me out!'

Papa Moll

Avast, me Hearties!

1 'This chaotic traffic mess,
   is all my fault, I must confess.'
   Papa Moll starts on the spot,
   untangling this traffic knot.

2 While Papa tries to make it right,
   the children see a brand new sight.
   'Look! Over there's a harbour pool,
   with a boat! Oh, wow! How cool!'

3 The whole boat is really swaying,
   full of many children playing.
   It looks like each kid has a ton
   of good old fashioned pirate fun!

4 Willy shows a hat to Fritz.
He even found one here that fits!
'Now Captain Willy is my name!
Come on, let's play a pirate game!'

5 Fritz says, 'Look! They've got swords too!
One for me, and one for you!
'We'll be pirates feared and cruel,
come on, let's have a sword fight duel!'

6 'I see foes behind us, look,
prepare to cast the grappling hook!'
Now Captain Willy grabs a rope.
His enemies have got no hope!

7 'I can catch them easily
with a lasso, just watch me.'
He swings the loop above his head,
'I'll capture them, alive or dead!'

8 'Ha!' shouts Willy with great joy,
half pirate and half cowboy.
Fritz is really quite impressed.
He thinks his brother is the best.

9 Look what Captain Willy's caught!
He really gave all that he's got.
His performance was tip top:
he's captured his own Mom and Pop!

Papa Moll

The Race

1 Here's a contest with a real,
genuine, old steamboat wheel.
All they have to do is row,
To see who's fast and who is slow!

2 'Papa, do you want to try?
You can do it, don't be shy!'
'I don't think that I'm fit enough'
says Moll, 'that really looks quite tough!'

3 Mama says 'This much is true,
I think that I'm more fit than you!'
Fritz claps his hands and calls: 'Let's see
who is stronger physically!'

4 Now four Molls all take a seat.
Each one is prepared to beat
that steamboat wheel quite easily.
See them smile expectantly.

5 As they await the race's start,
Moll feels the beating of his heart.
'I'll be the winner here, all right!
You can't beat me, try as you might!'

6 They hear the signal now to: 'Go!'
Moll shoots forwards like a pro,
and throws himself upon the line
with all his weight: 'This race is mine!'

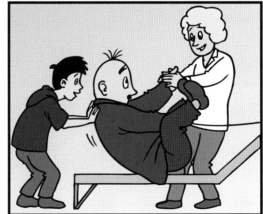

7 Poor Moll! That's not the way to win,
it's merely the way to fall in!
He flips around, his legs are waving.
Looks like Papa Moll needs saving.

8 Like a turtle on his shell,
things for Moll aren't going well.
With family cooperation,
another rescue operation.

9 Papa Moll must bite his lip.
'There is no way to beat that ship!'
'No, my Sweet, that's surely true'
said Mama, 'but I sure beat you!'

Papa Moll

Swissarena

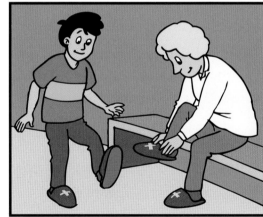

1 Right next door in the same hall,
   filling the floor from wall to wall,
   all Switzerland from left to right:
   a photo from a satellite.

2 'Come on, let us all go around
   and try to locate our hometown!'
   Who will be the first to spy it?
   All the Molls now want to try it!

3 If you want to walk in there,
   felt slippers are what you must wear!
   Mama is a little grumpy
   'I don't like them, they are frumpy!'

4   'We haven't found our hometown yet,
I'll find it first! You wanna bet?'
The map has neither word nor name,
to find home is a searching game.

5   They crawl around on hands and knees.
Each wants to be the first who sees
where they live, and so they look
in each Swiss valley, hill and brook.

6   When finally they find their city,
on the map, it's itsy-bitsy!
So tiny is each house and street,
their whole town looks so cute and sweet.

7   As they are crawling on the ground,
they all cry out: 'Look what I've found!'
And then a bang! Another shout:
they've nearly knocked each other out!

8   Who was the first? It's hard to tell,
after that head bang, crash and yell.
Says Papa Moll 'It seems to me,
that we won as a family!'

9   'Now that was quite a test to take,
it gave us all a big headache!'
says Papa Moll and rubs his head,
the others laugh at what he said!

Papa Moll

VIP Passenger

1 Between the buildings south and north,
both east and west and back and forth,
one sees mini wagons move,
the Molls wholeheartedly approve.

2 They wait their turn to sit and ride
along the mini tracks to glide.
The mini train now stops and waits,
but there's one man who hesitates.

3 They are small and they are narrow,
equal to a gnome's wheel barrow.
Papa Moll cannot decide
if he really fits inside.

4 'Toot!', there is a strict timetable,
   Moll climbs in while he's still able!
   First the train is puffing slow,
   but suddenly you see it go!

5 At the end of this round trip,
   it seems that Moll gave them the slip.
   In fact, his wagon's gone as well.
   What happenend here? No one can tell!

6 Then far away along the track,
   they see that Moll is coming back.
   He has to push his wagon now,
   'I guess it disengaged somehow!'

7 The locomotive driver cries
   'Oh no, I can't believe my eyes!
   How could I leave some one behind?
   I'm sorry Sir, that was not kind!'

8 To make up for this mistake
   Moll again is asked to take
   a special ride as VIP,
   around the whole vicinity!

Papa Moll

The Wild Flight

1 The next thing they want to see
   is aviation history!
   All the old things that once flew,
   airplanes, gliders, rockets too!

2 Flying objects from the past,
   with wings and strings and rocket's blast!
   So many ways to ride the breeze:
   people really flew in these!

3 The boys discover something great:
   'Look! Now we can simulate
   an airplane flight while on the ground,
   with real live video and sound!'

4 Moll is buckled in quite tight
in preparation for his flight.
The handle in his hands seems real.
Says Willy: 'Dad, how does it feel?'

5 The cockpit swerves and sinks and tilts,
Moll feels all the bumps and jilts.
All that happens can be seen
on the simulator's screen.

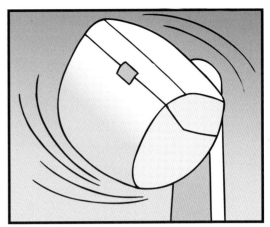

6 The flight begins with a big jolt,
they take off like a lightening bolt.
Then the flight gets really wild,
Willy is a fearless child!

7 Loop the loop, around they roll,
it's all too much for Papa Moll.
Willy doesn't seem to care,
he loves to play up in the air!

8 Inside this mad flying machine
sits Papa Moll. He's turning green!
Soon they've landed on the ground,
Papa Moll can't make a sound.

9 To take a break they're really ready,
neither one is looking steady.
Papa Moll croaks to his wife:
'That was the worst flight of my life!'

Papa Moll

Natural Talent

1   Before you join the cabin crew
there's a trick you have to do:
Here's a sense of balance test
to show who is above the rest!

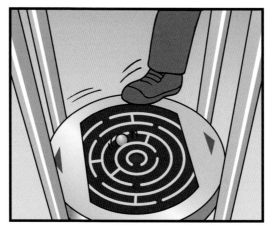

2   Fritz, of course, gives it a try.
After all, he loves to fly!
With his legs he needs to steer
the ball along the paths in here.

3   But this is no easy game,
Fritz gives up, says 'What a shame!
Papa with your wobbly knees:
you can do this in a breeze!'

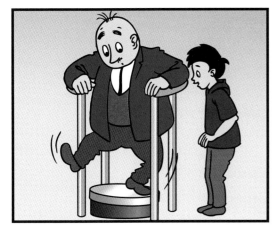

45

4 'There is a way, there is a will!'
Papa's knees are trembling still.
After that mad, crazy flight
he can't stand straight, try as he might.

5 He won't give up, 'I'll get this yet!'
says Papa Moll, 'You all can bet
that soon the ball will reach its goal,
or my name isn't Papa Moll!'

6 'Look how I can move this thing!'
laughs Papa Moll, the disco king!
'I was pale and feeling sickly,
I recovered really quickly!'

7 As Moll from the test descends
almost sad as the fun ends,
he says 'it was as delightful
as that flight was truly frightful'.

8 In the middle sits the ball.
Poor Fritz can't trust his eyes at all!
'Look what my old man just did!
He steered that ball right through the grid!'

9 'So you see,' said the old man,
'You never know, just what you can
do if you put your mind to it.
So I say: ,Don't wait, just do it!''

Papa Moll

Stargazer

1 Ever since we learned to fly,
began the conquest of the sky,
Mankind has reached up for the stars
from Earth to Moon and on to Mars!

2 To view the sky from earthly home,
they built a special indoor dome
on which all the stars projected,
galaxies can be inspected.

3 Now the show's set to begin,
and family Moll's just settled in.
They're excited, and quite soon
they see each planet, star and moon!

6 When the room is light again,
Papa Moll can feel a pain
in his neck from all that staring
at the dome. His pain is glaring.

4 When the planetarium
gets dark they see all the stars come
to life and move across the sky
All five Molls exclaim: 'Oh my!'

5 The stars seem close enough to touch.
The Molls enjoy this very much.
This really is a show of shows.
The room is filled with 'Ahs' and 'Ohs!'

7 'Ow, it hurts', poor Papa growls.
'Let me see, now stop your yowls'
says Mama, 'now just let me check',
and gently rubs his aching neck.

Papa Moll

In the Media Factory

1   The next room where the Molls all go:
    the television studio!
    Here is where TV is made,
    complete with all tricks of the trade.

2   Some visitors make their own show
    in the TV studio.
    The three kids all wonder how
    they could make their own show now.

3 And so it came that Mama Moll
begins a new show to extoll:
'Please let me introduce to you
a magic man whose powers are true.'

4 Papa Moll, the magic man
has got a tricky little plan.
He has the kids dress up in green
before he puts them in the scene.

5 Why did he choose those clothes so green?
Because on film they can't be seen!
And then begins the juggling show
with only heads, nothing below.

6 There's a screen upon the wall
of the museum's entrance hall.
The people who are standing there
all watch the juggling show and stare.

7 The talented magician's show
is met with shouts of: 'Great!' 'Bravo!'
'It's something new!'. He juggles heads
not balls but laughing kids instead.

8 In the end, Fritz sits and edits
the whole show from start to credits.
But how can he get the job done
with constant tips from everyone?!

Papa Moll

Papa Moll the Acrobat

1 'See Sky Jumpers bounce with glee?
   There's a space for you and me! '
   Fritz and Willy go in haste.
   'This is great! No time to waste!'

2 Strapped in tight, they bounce around.
   Bursts of laughter do abound.
   'It's so easy, without trying',
   Willy squeals, 'It's just like flying!'

3 Evi sees them bounce and drop.
   'I want to try! Come with me, Pop?'
   'If little Evi is not scared,'
   thinks Moll, 'I'll try. I am prepared!'

4   Evi's glad that Papa dares
    to jump despite the people's stares.
    He thinks that he will start off slow,
    and gather speed to really go.

5   Moll starts to jump most carefully.
    Up and down for all to see.
    Then in a flash, he's on his back;
    flipped right over with a smack!

6   He tries to right himself and then
    flips on over twice again!
    Now poor Moll looks on with dread,
    He's bouncing now upon his head!

7   Up and down, with daring twirls,
    Papa Moll through the air whirls,
    Like a crazy acrobat
    in the air and on the mat.

8   He thought the people would be mean
    because he had caused such a scene.
    But all the people clapped and cheered.
    They found him funny, but not weird.

9   'A circus number?' people ask.
    'Fancy jumps are quite a task'.
    'I think that it's enough today.
    Tomorrow we'll come back and play'.

Papa Moll

Almost Too Real

1   What a wonder it would be,
    Living deep beneath the sea.
    The kids ask, 'Papa can we go,
    to see the 3-D movie show?'

2   They rush inside and sit right down;
    excited people all around.
    A special film, that offers more.
    Moll asks, 'What are these glasses for?'

3   The glasses are a funny sight:
    'Is the screen small? The film too bright?'
    The others say, 'Wait, you will see,
    just how real this film will be!'

4 The lights go down, the show begins.
Soon the room is filled with fins
and bubbles everywhere to see.
The people watch attentively.

5 Moll can't believe what he can see:
the coral sways, the fish swim free.
Starfish swarming everywhere:
Moll feels like they're in his hair.

6 It feels so real, just like he's there,
swimming with the fish so fair.
Squids and swordfish, whales galore.
This is amazing! He wants more!

7 Schools of fish, look at their classes!
All because of magic glasses.
In the deep they seem to dive;
it really looks like they're alive!

8 All at once Moll's joy is changed:
his feelings are quite rearranged.
He screams in terror, 'Over there!
The great white shark just bit the air!'

9 Walking out into the light,
Papa says, 'That was a fright!'
The children took his hands and then
said, 'Papa can we go again?'

Papa Moll

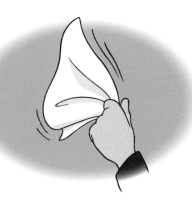

A Fond Farewell

1 With their visit near the end,
   It's time to fetch their furry friend.
   And while they wait for Chips to come,
   the kids can get some shopping done.

2 The souvenirs they find are great.
   So many, they can hardly wait!
   All kinds of gifts both big and small:
   from games to books, something for all!

3 A rocket ship caught Willy's eye,
   he wants to blast it to the sky!
   Evi has a thorough look
   and gets the latest Globi book.

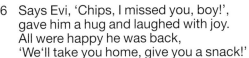

4   'Look who's coming down the hall'
    'Come here, you Rascal!' they all call.
    Chips is happy beyond measure;
    wags his tail with doggy pleasure.

5   When she lets Chips off the lead,
    he bounds to Molls with puppy speed.
    Wagging his tail, jumping around,
    yipping, yelping, like a clown.

6   Says Evi, 'Chips, I missed you, boy!',
    gave him a hug and laughed with joy.
    All were happy he was back,
    'We'll take you home, give you a snack!'

7   'Thanks, Ms Smith, for taking care'
    says Moll, 'while we had fun in there.'
    'Your dog is really very sweet,
    for me it was a welcome treat!'

8   Their museum visit now is done,
    they learned a lot and had such fun.
    Their minds filled up, their heads all swoon.
    Steiner says, 'We'll see you soon!'

9   'Soon, indeed' Moll answers him
    with a friendly parting grin.
    Sad to leave this learning treasure,
    coming back will be a pleasure.

Papa Moll

'Great Show, Mr Moll!'

1   All the doctors recommend
    sleeping long on the weekend.
    Moll works hard the whole week long,
    so snoozing later can't be wrong!

2   Dreams are shattered, sleepers wake
    when they hear the floorboards shake.
    Papa Moll opens his eyes:
    'It's too loud to sleep', he sighs.

3   Drowsily he stumbles down
    to find the source of this odd sound.
    Moll was snoozing, oh so deeply,
    and he's feeling still quite sleepy!

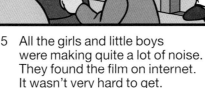

4   A group of kids, apparently,
    is watching Moll's show on TV.
    The juggling heads are what they see,
    they laugh and shout excitedly.

5   All the girls and little boys
    were making quite a lot of noise.
    They found the film on internet.
    It wasn't very hard to get.

6   'Your magic trick makes us all laugh,
    can we get your autograph?
    Mr Moll you are a star!
    We've all come from near and far!'

7   'The weather is quite nice today,
    why don't you kids go out and play?'
    'That would be a real great pleasure,
    we'll go out and look for treasure!'

8   'Good morning dear, no need to fear,
    the kids are up, that much is clear.
    But now they're out and having fun,
    with their friends out in the sun.'

9   'Outside I cannot hear a thing,
    except the morning birds who sing',
    says Mama Moll over her bread.
    'They're finding treasure', Papa said.

Papa Moll

Nearly New

1   Here they come with lots of stuff,
    it looks like they have found enough!
    Old toy boats and old toy planes,
    broken cars and rusty trains.

2   Their treasure-seeking expedition
    found only toys in bad condition.
    All are dirty, rusty, bent,
    with a hole, a rip or dent.

3   When they see what the kids took,
    their parents get a worried look.
    How could they bring home this big mess?
    It only means a lot more stress.

4 'Mama, Papa, don't complain!
Hear our plan, let us explain!
We saw the old things on display,
renovated all the way.'

5 'Like the museum renovates,
so can we', young Willy states.
Then they bid their friends goodbye.
'Come on. Let's give it a try!'

6 Papa Moll says: 'Let me see,
what can we fix here easily?
With patience and a little luck,
we'll fix each train, plane, ship and truck'.

7 Now they start with nail and screw,
hammer, drill and lots of glue.
They repair all that is worn,
each broken wheel, each wing that's torn.

8 With lots of renovation tricks,
the family could finally fix
and clean the toys so they looked new.
They really knew just what to do.

9 Papa smiles, full of pride
at these toys displayed outside.
They freed them from old rust and dirt.
Each Moll has traces on his shirt.

Papa Moll

Moll's own transport museum

1 Look what these Molls have created:
old junk toys now renovated!
Each screw is tight, the paint has dried.
Should they bring the toys inside?

2 Or should they try to sell the lot,
and put the money in a pot?
Or should they give it all away
for other kids who want to play?

3 Willy has a new position:
'We can make an exhibition!
Like we saw in old Lucerne
Transport Museum? Now it's our turn!'

4   The excitement is unbounded
    All the neighbours are astounded!
    The Molls have realized their dream,
    as family and as Museum Team!

At the beginning of this book, you can see the Moll family admiring three of the Swiss Transport Museum's most impressive objects. Here is some information to help you learn more about these fascinating vehicles.

The Unique Wooden Speedster

The Lockheed 9C Orion was the fastest passenger plane of the early 1930's. It had a seating capacity of five people, including the pilot, and a range of nearly 1000 kilometers. The 575 horsepower engine could propel the wooden airplane to a maximum speed of 360 km/h. The world's last remaining example is on exhibit at the Swiss Transport Museum.

The Heavyweight Legend

This heavy freight locomotive was built for mountain stretches on the Gotthard line. Officially called 'Be 6/8 II', it soon received the nickname 'Crocodile' due to its long, movable 'snout'. The Crocodile could master even the steepest, most winding climbs thanks to its 2240 horsepower. Thirty-three of these locomotives were built between 1920 and 1922. Thirteen Crocodiles, including the one in the Museum's collection, were modified to reach a maximum of 3640 horsepower. The last of these electric locomotives was in service at the Rhein Harbor in Basel until 1986.

Affordable Mass Production

The Ford Model T (pictured here is the delivery truck version, TT) was better known by its nickname, 'Tin Lizzy'. It was the first car to be manufactured on the assembly line. The customers were enthusiastic because this efficient production method lowered the sales price to about that of a motor scooter. Between 1908 and 1927 Ford built 15 million 'Tin Lizzies'.

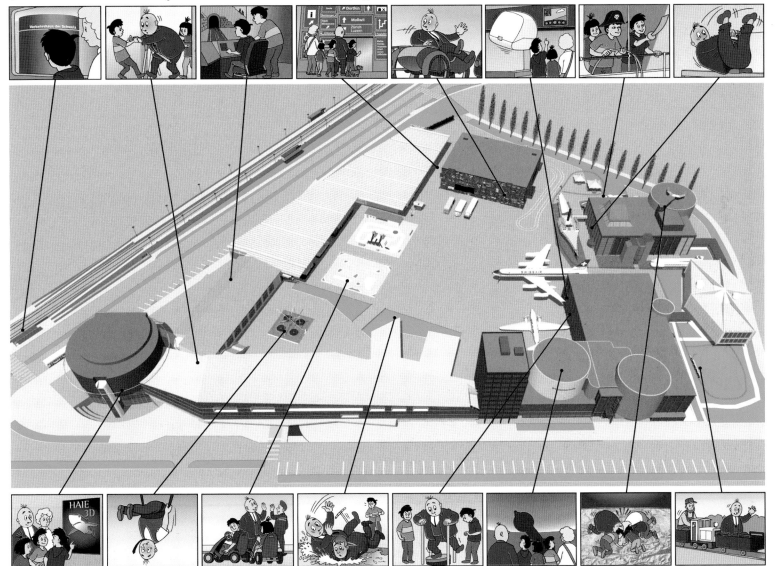

Papa Moll's
Swiss Museum of Transport Game

Do You know where all the stories are to be set?
Flip to the pages that fit to the location on this aerial view.